Easy Spanish Phrases for Kids

CHILDREN'S LEARN SPANISH BOOKS

BABY PROFESSOR

EDUCATION KIDS

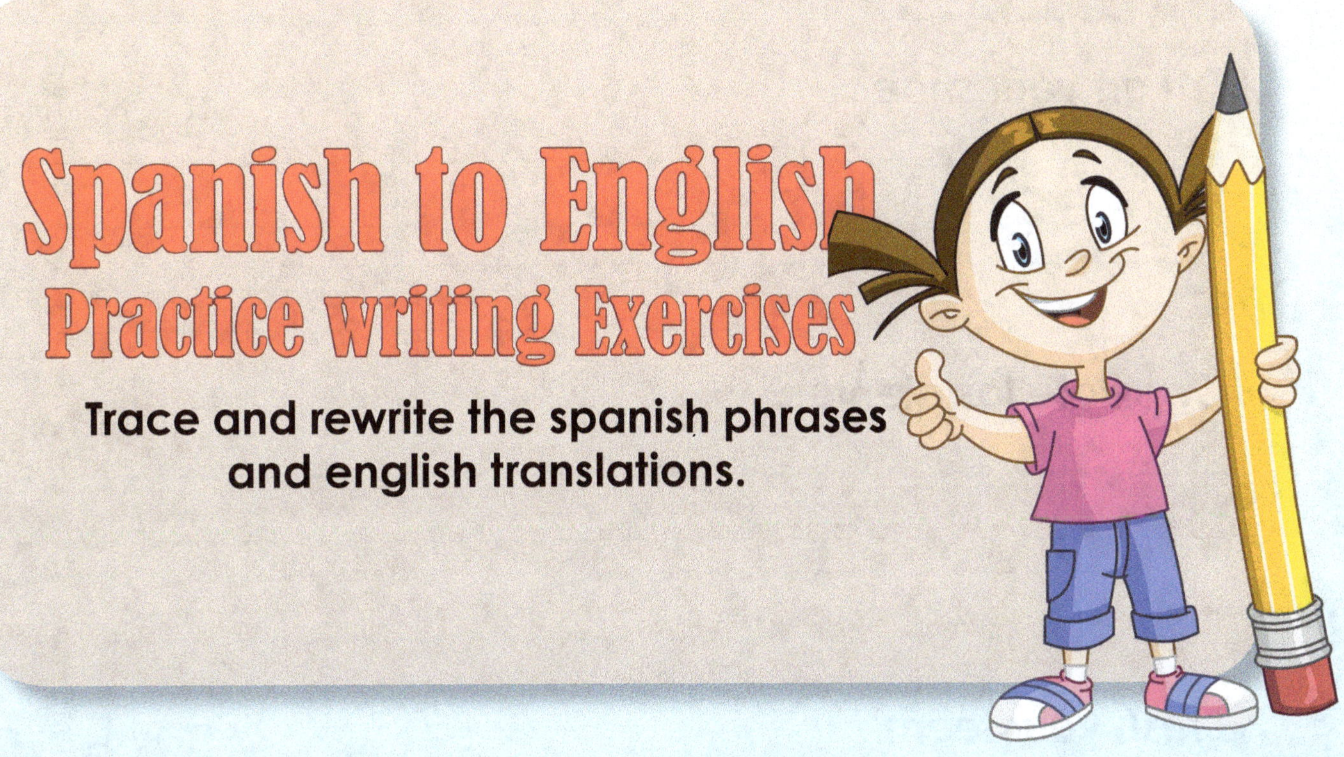

Spanish to English
Practice writing Exercises
Trace and rewrite the spanish phrases
and english translations.

¿hablas español?

Ponte los zapatos. Español

Ponte los zapatos.

Put on your shoes. English translation

Put on your shoes.

Cepíllate los dientes. Español

Cepíllate los dientes.

Brush your teeth. English translation

Brush your teeth.

Do you speak spanish?

Que descanses.

Que descanses.

Sleep well. (Sleep tight.)

Sleep well. (Sleep tight.)

Que sueñes con los angelitos.

Que sueñes con los angelitos.

Sweet dreams.

Sweet dreams.

¿hablas español?

Te adoro.

Te adoro.

I love you (I adore you).

I love you (I adore you).

Te quiero.

Te quiero.

I love you.

I love you.

Do you speak spanish?

¿Quieres agua?

¿Quieres agua?

Do you want some water?

Do you want some water?

Lávate las manos

Lávate las manos

Wash your hands.

Wash your hands.

¿hablas español?

Toma mi mano.

Toma mi mano.

Take my hand.

Take my hand.

Dame un abrazo.

Dame un abrazo.

Give me a hug.

Give me a hug.

Do you speak spanish?

Siéntate.

Siéntate.

Sit down.

Sit down.

Muy calladito/a por favor

Muy calladito/a por favor

Be really quiet.

Be really quiet.

¿hablas español?

Ven acá.

Ven acá.

Come here.

Come here.

No toques.

No toques.

Don't touch.

Don't touch.

Do you speak spanish?

Camina, por favor.   Español

Camina, por favor.

Walk, please.   English translation

Walk, please.

No corras.   Español

No corras.

Don't run.   English translation

Don't run.

¿hablas español?

Amárrate los zapatos

Amárrate los zapatos

Tie your shoes.

Tie your shoes.

Dime otra vez.

Dime otra vez.

Tell me again.

Tell me again.

Do you speak spanish?

Hazlo de nuevo

Hazlo de nuevo

Do it again.

Do it again.

¿Quieres leer?

¿Quieres leer?

Do you want to read a story?

Do you want to read a story?

¿hablas español?

¿Cuántos hay?

¿Cuántos hay?

How many are there?

How many are there?

¡Mira!

¡Mira!

Look.

Look.

Do you speak spanish?

Buenos días

Buenos días

Good morning

Good morning

¿Cómo amaneciste?

¿Cómo amaneciste?

How are you this morning?

How are you this morning?

¿hablas español?

Tenemos que irnos en….minutos *Español*

Tenemos que irnos en...minutos

We have to go in … minutes English translation

We have to go in ... minutes

Tiende la cama. *Español*

Tiende la cama.

Make your bed. English translation

Make your bed.

Do you speak spanish?

¿Te gusta?

¿Te gusta?

Do you like it?

Do you like it?

Me toca.

Me toca.

It's my turn.

It's my turn.

¿hablas español?

Te toca.

Te toca.

It's your turn.

It's your turn.

Cierra la puerta.

Cierra la puerta.

Close the door.

Close the door.

Do you speak spanish?

Apágalo.

Apágalo.

Turn it off.

Turn it off.

Pon la mesa

Pon la mesa

Set the table.

Set the table.

¿hablas español?

Ayúdame, por favor.

Español

Ayúdame, por favor.

Help me please.

English translation

Help me please.

¿Te ayudo?

Español

¿Te ayudo?

Can I help you?

English translation

Can I help you?

Do you speak spanish?

Por favor

Por favor

Please

Please

Gracias

Gracias

Thank you

Thank you

¿hablas español?

Bien hecho.

Bien hecho.

Well done.

Well done.

Intenta otra vez.

Intenta otra vez.

Try again.

Try again.

Do you speak spanish?

De nada

De nada

You're welcome.

You're welcome.

Con cuidado / Ten cuidado

Con cuidado / Ten cuidado

Be careful.

Be careful.

¿hablas español?

Guarda los juguetes

Guarda los juguetes

Pick up your toys.

Pick up your toys.

¿Acabaste?

¿Acabaste?

Are you done?

Are you done?

Do you speak spanish?

A la cama

A la cama

Time for bed.

Time for bed.

Apaga la luz.

Apaga la luz.

Turn off the light.

Turn off the light.

¿hablas español?

¿Dónde estás?

¿Dónde estás?

Where are you?

Where are you?

Ganaste.

Ganaste.

You won.

You won.

Do you speak spanish?

Gané.

Español

Gané.

I won.

English translation

I won.

Dame la mano.

Español

Dame la mano.

Give me your hand.

English translation

Give me your hand.

¿hablas español?

Me encanta.

Me encanta.

I love it.

I love it.

Lo haces bien.

Lo haces bien.

You do that well.

You do that well.

Do you speak spanish?

Lo hiciste bien.

Lo hiciste bien.

You did it really well.

You did it really well.

Me gusta

Me gusta

I like it.

I like it.

¿hablas español?

Es hora de dormir.

Es hora de dormir.

It's time to go to sleep.

It's time to go to sleep.

Es hora de ir a la cama.

Es hora de ir a la cama.

It's time for bed.

It's time for bed.

Do you speak spanish?

Buenas noches

Buenas noches

Español

Good night

Good night

English translation

¿Tienes hambre?

¿Tienes hambre?

Español

Are you hungry?

Are you hungry?

English translation

¿hablas español?

A comer

A comer

Come eat.

Come eat.

Es hora de comer

Es hora de comer

It's time to eat.

Are you hungry?

Do you speak spanish?

Come.

Come.

Eat.

Eat.

Cómetelo

Cómetelo

Eat it up.

Are you hungry?

¿hablas español?

¿Quieres más?

¿Quieres más?

Do you want more?

Do you want more?

Estoy tan contento

Estoy tan contento

I'm so glad

I'm so glad

Do you speak spanish?

Me comí el chocolate

Me comí el chocolate

I ate the chocolate

I ate the chocolate

Me encanta dibujar

Me encanta dibujar

I love to draw

I love to draw

¿hablas español?

Me haces feliz

Me haces feliz

You make me happy

You make me happy

Mi primer amor

Mi primer amor

My first love

My first love

Do you speak spanish?

Muchos te amo

Muchos te amo

I love you very much

I love you very much

No puedo vivir sin ti

No puedo vivir sin ti

I can't live without you

I can't live without you

¿hablas español?

Pienso en ti siempre

Pienso en ti siempre

I always think of you

I always think of you

Jugar basketball

Jugar basketball

Play basketball

Play basketball

Do you speak spanish?

Puedo color?

Puedo color?

Can I color it?

Can I color it?

Hola Maestro!

Hola Maestro!

Hi Teacher!

Hi Teacher!

Visit

BABY PROFESSOR
EDUCATION KIDS

www.BabyProfessorBooks.com
to download Free Baby Professor eBooks
and view our catalog of new and exciting
Children's Books